MODERN ROLE MODELS

Derek Jeter

Hal Marcovitz

Mason Crest Publishers

Produced by OTTN Publishing in association with
21st Century Publishing and Communications, Inc.

Copyright © 2009 by Mason Crest Publishers. All rights reserved. No part of this publication may be reproduced or transmitted in any form or by any means, electronic or mechanical, including photocopying, recording, taping, or any information storage and retrieval system, without permission from the publisher.

MASON CREST PUBLISHERS INC.
370 Reed Road
Broomall, Pennsylvania 19008
(866) MCP-BOOK (toll free)
www.masoncrest.com

Printed in the United States of America.

First Printing

9 8 7 6 5 4 3 2 1

Library of Congress Cataloging-in-Publication Data

Marcovitz, Hal.
  Derek Jeter / Hal Marcovitz.
    p. cm. — (Modern role models)
  Includes bibliographical references.
  ISBN-13: 978-1-4222-0482-5 (hardcover) — ISBN-13: 978-1-4222-0770-3 (pbk.)
  ISBN-10: 1-4222-0482-0 (hardcover)
 1. Jeter, Derek, 1974–   —Juvenile literature. 2.Baseball players—United States—Biography. I. Title.
 GV865.J48M37 2009
 796.357092—dc22
 [B]   2008020410

Publisher's note:
All quotations in this book come from original sources, and contain the spelling and grammatical inconsistencies of the original text.

CROSS-CURRENTS

*In the ebb and flow of the currents of life we are each influenced by many people, places, and events that we directly experience or have learned about. Throughout the chapters of this book you will come across **CROSS-CURRENTS** reference boxes. These boxes direct you to a **CROSS-CURRENTS** section in the back of the book that contains fascinating and informative sidebars and related pictures. Go on.* ▶▶

Prospect Heights Public Library
12 N. Elm Street
Prospect Heights, IL 60070
www.phpl.info

Contents

1 Most Valuable Player — 5

2 From Kalamazoo to New York City — 11

3 National Celebrity — 17

4 Rollercoaster Years — 27

5 Challenges Ahead — 37

Cross-Currents — 46

Chronology — 54

Accomplishments & Awards — 55

Further Reading & Internet Resources — 57

Glossary — 59

Notes — 61

Index — 63

Picture Credits — 64

About the Author — 64

Derek Jeter holds the MVP Trophy after the 2000 All-Star Game. During the July 11 game at Turner Field in Atlanta, Derek went three-for-three, including a double, at the plate. He drove in two key runs as the American League squad won the game, 6-3. Derek became the first Yankees player to be honored as All-Star MVP.

Most Valuable Player

WHEN DEREK JETER STEPPED TO THE PLATE IN the 2000 All-Star Game at Turner Field in Atlanta, Georgia, he intended to show the baseball world that he deserved to start. It was Derek's third All-Star Game, but in his previous two appearances in the mid-summer classic, the New York Yankee **shortstop** started the game on the bench.

Derek had made the **American League** All-Star squad for the first time in 1998, his third season in the major leagues. That year, Derek played behind starter Alex Rodriguez of the Seattle Mariners. A year later, Derek was again selected for the American League squad, but watched Nomar Garciaparra of the Boston Red Sox open the game at shortstop. Derek eventually played in both games, but his performances were hardly impressive: two at-bats and two strikeouts.

⟐ A Chance to Start ⟐

For the 2000 game, Rodriguez was again voted in by the fans to start

DEREK JETER

at shortstop, but an injury kept him out of the lineup and cleared the way for Derek to make his first start in an All-Star lineup. Derek intended to make the most of his opportunity.

Facing Randy Johnson of the Arizona Diamondbacks in the first **inning**, Derek stroked a double to left field. In the third, he singled off Los Angeles Dodgers pitcher Kevin Brown, then scored the first run of the game when Brown gave up a bases-loaded walk. In the fourth, Derek hit a single off Al Leiter of the New York Mets that scored two runs, giving his squad a 3-1 lead over the **National League**. The game ended in a 6-3 American League victory. When reporters crowded around Derek after the game, the shortstop said his plan had been to come out swinging, no matter who was pitching:

> **"I basically had the same game plan against everyone. I'm a free swinger. I think it's known around the league, maybe both leagues. I wanted to at least put the ball in play. But when you're facing guys like that, you want to swing early in the count. If you fall behind, you're in trouble."**

Derek's performance earned him selection as the game's Most Valuable Player. Incredibly, in the 71-year history of the mid-summer classic, Derek Jeter was the first Yankee player to earn the honor. None of the great Yankee **immortals**—Babe Ruth, Lou Gehrig, Joe DiMaggio, Mickey Mantle, Reggie Jackson, and Dave Winfield, among others—had ever been voted All-Star MVP.

✦ PRODUCING WITH BAT AND GLOVE ✦

In Major League Baseball, teams in the American and National leagues meet only a handful of times each season until the American League champion plays the National League champion in the World Series. In the fall of 2000, the Yankees won the American League pennant while the Mets captured the National League title. The fact that both teams played in New York added drama to the match-up because a "**Subway** Series" is rare in baseball.

In the first game, played at Yankee Stadium, Derek walked and scored in the sixth inning.

CROSS-CURRENTS

For background information on other World Series played by two teams from the same city, read "The Subway Series." Go to page 46. ▸▸

Most Valuable Player

Derek was pictured scoring a run during the 2000 World Series on the cover of *Sports Illustrated*. Derek hit a robust .409 during the five-game Series against the Mets. His nine hits included two doubles, a triple, and a home run. Derek scored six runs, more than any other player during the Subway Series.

In the field, he made a crucial play when he fielded a fly in shallow left, then rifled an off-balance throw home to nail speedy Timo Perez at the plate. The game was tied at that point, meaning that Derek's

DEREK JETER

Avoiding a sliding opponent, Derek turns a double play during the 2000 season. Although the Yankees shortstop is better known for his ability to get on base and score runs, his defensive skills also deserve respect. Derek has made many big plays in the field—often when a game is on the line.

Most Valuable Player

play foiled the Mets' attempt to take the lead. The game didn't end till the twelfth inning, when Tino Martinez scored off a single by Jose Vizcaino, giving the Yankees a 4-3 win.

In game two, Derek picked up three hits and scored a run in the eighth inning, which turned out to be pivotal. Heading into the ninth, the Mets were behind 6-0, but they picked up five runs before their rally fell short.

As the Series unfolded, Derek continued to produce with his bat and glove. But game three was the big one because it was a home game for the Mets. Recalling how it felt to walk onto the turf in Shea Stadium, the Mets' home field, Derek said,

> **"Going into Shea Stadium during the Series wasn't anything like walking on the field during interleague play. Even though we had been to the Series many times before, the intensity level at Shea was unbelievable."**

But the Mets won the third game, 4-2. Derek had two hits and scored a run in the loss. In the fourth game, also played at Shea Stadium, Derek homered to open the game. He added a triple in the third and later scored in the Yankees' 3-2 win. In the fifth game, Derek faced Leiter for the first time since the All-Star Game. He delivered a home run in the sixth, and the Yankees won 4-2, taking the World Series four games to one.

Derek's performances, providing key plays or hits in every Yankees win, earned him Most Valuable Player honors. In winning the award, he became the first player in baseball history to win MVP of the Series and the All-Star Game in the same year. Said Derek,

> **"Winning the MVP award after we had prevailed in game five was really an added bonus, and also an incredible honor. Players don't ever think about being named MVP. Basically, our goal is to get through the season successfully, make it to the postseason, play in the World Series, and win."**

From a young age, Derek Jeter wanted to play in the major leagues. His parents later said that, when he was eight, Derek told them that he wanted to play for the New York Yankees one day. After an outstanding high school baseball career, the Yankees chose Derek with the team's first pick in the 1992 baseball draft.

2

From Kalamazoo to New York City

YOUNG DEREK JETER DREAMED OF BASEBALL, and the Yankees were always part of the dream. In fourth grade, he told his teacher that the Yankees were his favorite team and later wrote that his career goal was to play for the Yankees. In art class, for a project designing a family **coat of arms**, Derek drew a Yankee at bat.

Derek's parents—Charles, a social worker, and Dorothy, an accountant—never discouraged their son from harboring such lofty ambitions. They told him that with hard work, he could accomplish anything. And they were willing to work with their son to help him achieve his ambitions. Starting when Derek was very young, Charles would hit him ground balls so the boy could learn how to field. His younger sister, Sharlee, helped by fielding Derek's throws. Even Dorothy would help with practice, pitching wiffle balls to Derek. Derek recalls those early days and the love he got from his family:

DEREK JETER

> "My mother and father are an amazing couple. Generous, intelligent, caring, supportive, proud, demanding. . . . I can't recall ever witnessing a set of parents who have been more devoted and more supportive to their two children than my mom and dad have been to me and my sister, Sharlee."

Natural Talent

Derek Sanderson Jeter was born on June 26, 1974, in Pequannock, a New Jersey town not far from New York City. But Derek would not get the opportunity to grow up among other Yankee fans. When he was four years old, Derek and his family moved to the small Michigan city of Kalamazoo, where his father pursued a doctoral degree at nearby Western Michigan University. Derek would spend the remainder of his childhood in Kalamazoo.

He attended St. Augustine Cathedral School in Kalamazoo and later Kalamazoo Central High School. From the start, he impressed his teachers with his intelligence, ambition, and leadership skills. He made friends easily with people of all ethnic backgrounds, which is easy to understand since Derek's father is African American and his mother is white.

One time, though, a teacher told Charles and Dorothy that Derek had been cruel to a classmate. The Jeters sat their son down and told him that was unacceptable conduct—that he should treat people the way he expected them to treat him. The Jeters could tell that Derek took their words to heart. Said Chris Oosterbaan, one of Derek's teachers at St. Augustine,

> **CROSS-CURRENTS**
> For some history about the experiences of people of mixed racial backgrounds in the United States, read "Multiracial Americans." Go to page 47.

> "He was pretty much head and shoulders above his contemporaries, but he never came across as being arrogant. He didn't paint a glowing picture of himself and he didn't have this 'I'm really cool' attitude. He was very genuine and humble."

At Kalamazoo Central, Derek took his classroom work very seriously. He earned a 3.87 grade-point average, just below a perfect 4.0. He was also secretary of the school's National Honor Society and served as president of the Latin club. As for Derek's skills on the

From Kalamazoo to New York City

baseball field, he soon showed his talent as a natural athlete and excelled as a player. In his junior year at Kalamazoo Central, he hit .557 and swatted seven homers. He started drawing the interest of Major League scouts. A year later, after collecting a number of honors—including designation by *USA Today* as High School Player of the Year—he was selected by the Yankees with the sixth overall pick in that year's draft. Derek also received an athletic **scholarship** offer from the University of Michigan. But his desire to play professional baseball for his favorite team was too great. He passed up college and accepted the Yankees' offer, signing a $700,000 **contract**.

> **CROSS-CURRENTS**
> If you would like to learn more about Derek Jeter's hometown in Michigan, check out "Kalamazoo." Go to page 48.

"Like a Colt"

Soon after graduating from high school in 1992, Derek joined the Yankees **farm system**, playing for minor league teams in Tampa, Florida, and Greensboro, North Carolina. His first year in professional baseball was hard. Homesick, Derek spent most of his time in Tampa in his hotel room, running up monthly phone bills of $400 calling home to Kalamazoo. Meanwhile, he hit a dismal .202 in Tampa, going 0-for-14 in his first 14 at-bats. In Greensboro, his production at the plate improved only slightly, and he finished the season with a .243 average.

Still, team insiders saw Derek as a diamond in the rough. Clete Boyer, a former Yankee infielder who worked with Derek that first year, said,

> "He's like a colt. He's got that raw ability. You just have to do it to get the smoothness you need. He's hearing things he's never heard before. He's got quite a ways to go."

Derek's 1993 season proved to be bumpy as well, particularly in the field. Playing the entire year in Greensboro, he committed fifty-six errors in 126 games. His batting average improved, though, and he finished the season with a .295 average. He was also selected for the South Atlantic League All-Star Team.

The Yankees promoted him in 1994. He started the season with a minor league club in Tampa and moved up to Albany, New York, in mid-season. He ended the year playing for the Yankees' top farm club in Columbus, Ohio, a AAA team that competes on a level just below

DEREK JETER

This trading card pictures Derek in his Kalamazoo Central High School uniform. Derek was good enough to win a spot on the high-school team as a freshman, and batted over .500 in both his junior and senior years. Those stats were good enough to make him the first high-school player selected in the 1992 draft.

Major League competition. Derek knew they expected a lot from him:

> **"The Yankees, who had been very careful about promoting players through the system quickly, broke that routine with me. They kept challenging me and I kept succeeding, knocking aside goals as I moved from level to level."**

Derek spent one more year in the minors. In fact, soon after the 1995 season started, he was briefly called up to the Yankees, playing in fifteen Major League games before returning to Columbus for the remainder of the season. On opening day in 1996, he took his place on the field as the Yankees' starting shortstop.

Rookie of the Year

In his **rookie** year, Derek fulfilled the promise that had convinced the Yankees to select him sixth overall in the 1992 draft. On opening day, he hit a home run against the Cleveland Indians, then made a spectacular over-the-shoulder catch in the field. Early in the season, Yankees manager Joe Torre said he hoped his rookie shortstop would hit .250. By the end of the year, Derek had surpassed Torre's expectations, hitting .314. He struggled a bit on defense, committing 22 errors. Still, the baseball world was awed by his talent. He was selected 1996 American League Rookie of the Year, picked unanimously by the baseball **journalists** who vote for the award.

Derek's play helped the Yankees win a postseason berth. That fall, the Yankees played the Baltimore Orioles for the American League pennant. In the opening game of the series, Derek found himself part of one of the most controversial plays of the year.

Coming to the plate in the eighth inning at Yankee Stadium, with Baltimore ahead 4-3, Derek lofted a ball deep into right field, sending Orioles outfielder Tony Tarasco to the wall. It appeared as if Tarasco would have a play on the ball. Tarasco drifted back to snag the ball and end the Yankees' threat. But just as Tarasco leaped for the ball, a Yankee fan reached over with his mitt, deflecting the ball into the stands.

Under the rules, Derek should have been called out due to fan interference, but the umpire did not see the interference and called the ball a home run. Derek circled the bases to tie the game and, in the eleventh inning, the Yankees scored the winning run. Later, the Yankees went on to defeat the Atlanta Braves in the World Series.

SHORT STORY

DEREK JETER AND ALEX RODRIGUEZ HEAD UP THE FINEST GROUP OF SHORTSTOPS SINCE WORLD WAR II

Before Derek's second season, 1997, he was pictured on the cover of *Sports Illustrated* with another young shortstop, Alex Rodriguez of the Seattle Mariners. The two young players—both were under 23 years old at the time—emerged as the best shortstops in the American League during the 1996 season.

National Celebrity

AFTER WINNING ROOKIE OF THE YEAR HONORS in 1996, Derek Jeter continued to chalk up impressive statistics. In 1997 he played in 159 games, hitting a sold .291 with 10 home runs and 116 runs scored. The Yankees again reached the playoffs, but lost in the first round to the Cleveland Indians.

The next season Derek hit .324 with 19 home runs as the Yankees emerged as the best team in baseball. New York set a league record with 114 wins in the regular season, and went on to win the World Series. In mid-season Derek was selected to the All-Star team for the first time. At the end of the year he finished third in the balloting for the league's Most Valuable Player.

New Contracts

By now, Derek was one of baseball's biggest stars—and he would soon be richly compensated for his talent. Shortly before the 1999 season, the Yankees offered to raise Derek's salary to $3.2 million a year. Derek refused the offer and sought intervention by a panel of arbitrators—an independent, three-person board retained by Major League Baseball to resolve salary disputes. The arbitrators convened a hearing and, after weighing Derek's value to the team, decided the Yankees should pay their shortstop $5 million a year.

Derek soon showed he was worth the new contract. In 1999, he hit a career-best .349. He finished with the second-highest batting average in the American League, behind Boston's Nomar Garciaparra, who hit .357. But the Yankees had the last laugh, as they beat the Red Sox in the playoffs and went on to win another World Series title. In 2000 Derek hit .339 with 15 homers during the regular season and the Yankees defeated the Mets in the Subway Series. Since Derek had joined the team, the Yankees had won the World Series five times in six seasons.

The Yankees' shortstop would soon ink an even bigger deal. In February 2001, Derek prepared to report to the Yankees' spring training headquarters in Florida to begin the final year under his 1999 contract. Following the 2001 season, Derek would become a free agent—available to sign a contract with any Major League team. When players put themselves on the market as free agents, they can often attract lucrative offers as many teams bid for their services.

But before spring training, Yankees owner George Steinbrenner stepped in and offered Derek a contract that would keep him off the free agent market. Under Derek's new contract, the Yankees agreed to pay their shortstop a total of $189 million over the next ten years. It was the second-largest contract in the history of Major League Baseball. Only Alex Rodriguez of the Texas Rangers had been awarded a larger contract—his deal called for payments totaling $252 million over ten years. Said Steinbrenner,

> **CROSS-CURRENTS**
> *To learn how Derek and others benefited financially from the sacrifices of earlier ballplayers, read "Baseball's High Salaries." Go to page 49.*

> **"** Derek Jeter embodies everything the Yankees are about. There are some things that cannot be defined by batting average, home runs and runs batted in. Equally important are an athlete's heart and desire. **"**

> **CROSS-CURRENTS**
> *To learn why the Yankees' owner is known as a tough person to work for, read "George Steinbrenner—Always the Boss." Go to page 50.*

National Celebrity

Derek runs the bases during a World Series game. During Derek's first five seasons with the Yankees, the team won the World Series four times. Derek was a big part of the team's postseason success. In 61 playoff games between 1996 and 2000, Derek hit .324 and scored 48 runs.

DEREK JETER

Derek said he was stunned by the amount of money the Yankees offered him—and also grateful that he would be able to continue his career in New York:

> **"I really felt there was no reason to see if the grass was greener on the other side. Even if I had played out the year, my first choice would have been New York. I never intended to play elsewhere, and to be honest with you, never intended to look elsewhere."**

Baseball History

Derek proved himself worthy of the fat contract. In 2001, he put together another solid year at the plate, hitting .311 and leading his team back to the World Series. One major achievement that season, though, came in the field, not at the plate. That October, during the third game of the divisional playoff series against the Oakland Athletics, the Yankees were holding onto a 1-0 lead in the seventh inning. At the time, the Yankees trailed in the series two games to none, meaning that if the A's won the third game, the Yankees would be eliminated from postseason play.

With the Athletics' Jeremy Giambi on first, Terrence Long hit a hard liner into the right field corner. Yankees outfielder Shane Spencer retrieved the ball and fired it hard over the heads of Alfonso Soriano and Tino Martinez, both of whom had taken positions to cut off the throw and relay it home. Meanwhile, Giambi was rounding the bases. As Giambi approached third base, A's coach Ron Washington waved him home.

Spencer's throw was heading toward the first-base dugout, and Giambi should have scored easily. But out of nowhere, it seemed, Derek suddenly reached out to snare the errant throw. He had been guarding third base during the play, but out of instinct drifted across the infield where, as it turned out, he was in perfect position to field Spencer's throw. He flipped the ball quickly to catcher Jorge Posada. If Giambi had known the ball was still in play, he probably would have slid into home. Instead, as he stayed on his feet down the base path, Posada nipped him on the back of the right leg a split-second before he crossed the plate. Umpire Kerwin Danley made the call: out at home. The Yankees dugout exploded.

National Celebrity

Derek turns a double play during a 2001 playoff game against the Oakland A's. The shortstop's solid defense—in particular, a key play during the third game of the American League Divisional Series—helped New York come back to win the playoff series in five games. Derek also contributed at the plate, batting .444 against Oakland.

The play—which sportswriters dubbed "The Flip"—turned out to be one of the key plays of the 2001 baseball season. *USA Today* named it to its list of the top ten most amazing plays of all time. As for Derek, he admitted being a bit stunned by the attention given to the play. He told reporters that he had simply placed himself in a position to make a play on the ball. But Yankees pitcher Mike Mussina, who had given up the hit to Long, knew better. Mussina said,

> **"There are players in this league, in baseball, when you play with them every day, you get to see what they come up with. It can be as simple as running the bases or the play he made today."**

➤ Bittersweet Victory ⬅

Derek's play in the field helped the Yankees hold onto their lead. The team rallied in the series, beat the Athletics, and played its way into the World Series. For New Yorkers that fall, the Yankees' victory was bittersweet: only weeks before, a terrorist attack on New York City had destroyed the World Trade Center and killed approximately 2,700 people from 80 countries. A city wounded by the tragedy was able to find some comfort in the Yankees' success.

The 2001 World Series between the Yankees and Arizona Diamondbacks would turn out to be one of the most riveting Series in years. The series opened in Arizona, where the Diamondbacks easily won both games. Back in New York, the Yankees took the third game of the Series by a 2-1 score, thanks mostly to a strong pitching performance by Roger Clemens and three errors committed by Diamondbacks fielders.

In the fourth game, the Diamondbacks held a 3-1 lead after eight innings. In the bottom of the ninth, Derek tried to bunt his way to first, but he was thrown out by a step. Later in the inning, with two outs, Tino Martinez hit a two-run homer off Diamondbacks reliever Byung-Hyun Kim, tying the game. An inning later, Derek homered to give the Yankees the victory, tying the Series at two games each.

In the fifth game of the Series, which was played at Yankee Stadium, the Diamondbacks again held a lead in the ninth inning, but the Yankees tied the score and went on to win in the twelfth inning. Now, the Series headed back to Arizona, with the Yankees ahead three games to two.

Facing elimination, the Diamondbacks exploded in the sixth game, scoring 15 runs. In fact, the 22 hits collected by Diamondbacks players tied a World Series record. In the final game, the Yankees held a 2-1 lead in the ninth inning, getting the go-ahead run in the seventh when Derek, who had singled, scored on a hit by Martinez.

National Celebrity

But the Diamondbacks tied the score in the ninth and, with the bases loaded, Arizona outfielder Luis Gonzales lofted a soft blooper over Derek's head, scoring infielder Jay Bell and winning the Series for Arizona. Derek was gracious, saying after the game,

❝ **They kept battling and they deserved to be champions.** ❞

Millions of Americans tuned in for the third game of the 2001 World Series at Yankee Stadium. The emotional game was played less than two months after terrorists destroyed the World Trade Center in New York on September 11, 2001. Although the Yankees won the third game, the team ultimately lost the World Series in seven games.

DEREK JETER

⇒ GLARE OF PUBLICITY ⇐

Despite the sting of the World Series loss, Derek still managed to enjoy his status as one of the wealthiest athletes in the United States. His picture appeared on the covers of national magazines proclaiming him one of baseball's biggest stars. New York fans, known for their often abrasive attitudes, were particularly enthusiastic in their devotion to the Yankees' shortstop. Derek couldn't even go for a walk on a midtown Manhattan street without being mobbed by autograph

Fans clamor for Derek's autograph before a 2002 game. By this time, the all-star shortstop was one of the most popular ballplayers in the United States. Derek tried to keep stories about his personal life out of the pages of newspapers. However, he was unable to avoid articles that speculated about his romantic relationships.

seekers. He also found himself on the covers of the **tabloid** press, which took more interest in his romantic life than in his accomplishments on the field.

Since arriving in New York, Derek had been fiercely protective of his privacy. However, he did give the tabloids plenty to write about. Soon after he broke into the Major Leagues, Derek was rumored to be dating pop star Mariah Carey. Carey helped fuel those rumors when, shortly after her divorce from music producer Tommy Mottola in 1998, the singer showed up in Tampa, Florida, to watch Derek as he played in spring training games. The relationship continued into the season, and the press spotted Carey in the stands of several Major League ballparks.

By mid-season, however, the relationship was over. Derek blamed the glare of publicity for his breakup with Carey, saying,

> "It's hard for me to have a relationship the way things are right now. I'd have to be with someone very understanding, someone who's willing to deal with all the attention."

If Derek thought the media scrutiny of his private life would end, he was mistaken. Soon, the tabloids linked him with other beautiful stars, including Miss Universe Lara Dutta, actresses Scarlett Johannson, Jordana Brewster, Gabrielle Union, Jessica Alba, and Jessica Biel, model Adriana Lima, TV host Vanessa Minnillo, and singer Joy Enriquez. Still Derek tried his best to stay out of the spotlight.

The 2003 and 2004 seasons were frustrating for Derek and his teammates. In 2003, Derek suffered the first major injury of his career, and in 2004 he battled through a long batting slump. But Derek was more disappointed in the fact that the Yankees failed to win the World Series either year than he was with his on-field struggles.

4

Rollercoaster Years

DURING HIS FIRST EIGHT SEASONS WITH THE Yankees, Derek Jeter had rarely missed games because of injury or illness. He kept himself in top physical condition by exercising hard, particularly in the off-season at his home in Tampa, Florida. His dedication to fitness paid off. In most seasons, he played in 150 or more games per year.

But his resiliency suffered a setback in 2003. On opening day of the season, during a game against the Toronto Blue Jays, Derek drew a walk. Jason Giambi then stroked an easy grounder back to the mound, forcing Derek to run to second. Pitcher Roy Halladay fielded Giambi's hit, then tossed to first for the out. Derek would have been safe at second but, seeing a chance to steal third, he kept running and headed for the extra base. Catcher Ken Huckaby made it to third ahead of Derek and took the throw from the Blue Jays' Carlos Delgado.

DEREK JETER

Derek crashed hard into Huckaby, dislocating his right shoulder. His **humerus** was knocked out of the shoulder socket. It was an extremely painful injury. Jonathan Glashow, a New York City surgeon who specializes in treating dislocations, said:

> "A shoulder dislocation is very painful. It's a 10 on a scale of 1 to 10 when it first happens. You can't move your arm. You get numbness and tingling in your fingers. There's also a lot of bleeding under the skin."

The collision with Huckaby knocked Derek out of the game. Worse, it knocked him out of action for almost the next two months. He missed nearly 40 games—almost a quarter of the Yankees' season—before rejoining the team in late May.

The Captain

Without Derek in the lineup, the Yankees played some of their worst baseball in years. At one point in May, the team won just three of fifteen games. Off the field, Yankees owner George Steinbrenner fumed and manager Joe Torre struggled to find a winning formula.

When Derek returned from his injury, Steinbrenner took a bold step. He named Jeter Yankees' captain—a rare honor that has been given to only ten other Yankees in the long history of the team, including Babe Ruth, Lou Gehrig, Thurman Munson, Willie Randolph, and Graig Nettles. When Derek was named captain in 2003, the Yankees had been without an on-the-field leader since 1995, when All-Star first baseman Don Mattingly had retired. In naming Derek captain, Steinbrenner said that he was counting on the shortstop's leadership abilities to rally his team out of its slump. Yankees General Manager Brian Cashman told the press,

> "The reality in that clubhouse is, informally, people recognized [Derek] as the captain, anyway. Now the Boss has recognized him in a formal way, and that's a great honor."

Following Derek's appointment as captain and return to the field, the Yankees started playing better. The team shook off its slump and

Rollercoaster Years

Derek talks with his teammates during a 2003 playoff game against the Boston Red Sox. The Yankees' captain showed his leadership ability by helping the team rally during the playoffs. Down three games to one and facing elimination, the Yankees took three straight games from the Red Sox to reach the World Series for the sixth time in eight years.

got back in the divisional race. Derek recovered from the effects of his shoulder injury and compiled good numbers for the year, hitting .324 with 87 runs scored in 119 games. The team won its division and eventually the pennant. The American League Championship Series against the rival Boston Red Sox was particularly exciting. It included two emotional bench-clearing brawls in which several

DEREK JETER

In 2003, Derek continued to prove that he was one of the best hitters in the American League. Although he missed more than a month of the season with a serious injury, he finished with a .324 batting average. That was the third-best average in the league, just behind batting champ Bill Mueller (.326) and Manny Ramirez (.325).

players from both teams were fined. Down three games to one, the Yankees came back to win in dramatic fashion, winning the seventh game on an 11th-inning home run by third baseman Aaron Boone.

Overall, though, 2003 ended on a sour note for the Yankees. In the World Series, the Yankees lost in six games to the Florida Marlins. The loss was particularly devastating to Derek, whose play in the sixth game contributed to the team's loss. In the fifth inning, with the tying run on

CROSS-CURRENTS

For information about the competition between the Yankees and the Red Sox, check out "The Hottest Sports Rivalries." Go to page 51. ▶▶

second base, Derek came to the plate but went down swinging on a 97 mile per hour fastball by Marlins pitcher Josh Beckett. In the sixth inning, Derek fielded a routine ground ball hit by the Marlins' Jeff Conine, but made a late throw that allowed Conine to reach first. It was the first fielding error Derek had ever committed in the 27 World Series games he had played. Conine scored later in the inning on a **sacrifice fly**, giving the Marlins an insurance run. After the game, Derek found it hard to accept the loss. He said,

> "There's no way you can rate losing. You either lose or you win. It's not like we lost less this time. Win or lose, it's pretty much black and white."

The Dive

Derek's botched play in the sixth game of the 2003 World Series added fuel to complaints that he had been hearing from his critics for years—that he simply was not a very good fielder. Even winning the Gold Glove—baseball's highest award for fielding—in 2004 and later years would not silence the critics.

ESPN Page 2 columnist Jeff Merron included Derek on his list of the 10 most overrated athletes. Wrote Merron,

> "Jeter's good. Very good. Probable Hall of Famer. But his performance has declined every year since 1999, and he's only the fourth-best shortstop in the American League. Defensively? Adequate, at best."

Derek heard that type of criticism even though he continued to make big plays in the field. In July 2003, a game against the Boston Red Sox had gone into extra innings. By the twelfth inning, the teams were tied at three runs each. In the top of the twelfth, the Red Sox put together a scoring threat with runners at second and third. Red Sox outfielder Trot Nixon then lofted a high fly ball toward the third base stands. The ball appeared to be drifting foul, but Derek dove for the fly, snagging it over his shoulder as he launched himself headfirst over the railing with fans scrambling to get out of his way. He hit the seats hard, but held onto the ball and made the out. In the next inning, the Red Sox scored a go-ahead run, but in the bottom of the thirteenth, the Yankees rallied to win. After the game, Derek was treated at a hospital for cuts on his face and a bruised shoulder. Yankees manager Joe Torre was stunned by the gutsy fielding play, which sportswriters labeled "The Dive." Torre's admiration for Derek was clear:

> **"Those are the things I keep saying, that don't show up in the stats. To make a play like that, with the game on the line, is pretty . . . special."**

Struggles at the Plate

While plays like "The Dive" helped his team win, in 2004 Derek struggled at the plate for the first time in his career. Derek started the 2004 season mired in a deep slump—through the end of May, his average hovered around the .190 mark, including an 0-for-32 skid in April and a 5-for-45 dry spell in May.

Before the 2004 season, Texas Rangers shortstop Alex Rodriguez had joined the Yankees, moving to third base so Derek could remain at shortstop. Rodriguez is the holder of baseball's biggest contract; under the pact, the Yankees paid him $27.5 million a year. Some sportswriters suggested that Derek's slump was more mental than physical—that Derek was troubled by Rodriguez's presence on the team. Torre defended his star player and said that Rodriguez's presence in the lineup had nothing to do with Derek's slump:

> **"I'd have to change my evaluation of Jeter if this is what's contributing to his bad year. We all have an ego, but he's never worried about someone else getting attention, because there's always someone every year coming on board to get attention. This kid, if that's the case, then I don't know him."**

Most baseball insiders expected Derek to eventually break out of his slump. In June, the hits started coming, and by the end of the year he finished with a respectable .292 average.

As for the Yankees, they won their division, but the season included a huge embarrassment—a 22-0 loss at the hands of the Cleveland Indians. No team in Yankee history had lost by such a wide margin. The loss also tied the Major League record—in 1975, the Chicago Cubs had fallen to the Pittsburgh Pirates by a 22-0 score.

Rollercoaster Years

Derek (right) talks with third baseman Alex Rodriguez between innings of a 2004 game. In the mid-1990s, Jeter and Rodriguez had been good friends. Their off-field relationship had cooled by the time Rodriguez joined the Yankees before the 2004 season. However, the two star players were able to work together well on the field.

DEREK JETER

Derek Jeter's batting slump during the early part of 2004 was so unusual, it was featured on the cover of *Sports Illustrated*. Eventually, Derek turned things around at the plate. He finished the year with a .292 batting average, 188 hits, 111 runs scored, a career-best 44 doubles, and 23 home runs.

Rollercoaster Years

Still, the Yankees made it to the postseason, only to lose to their longtime rivals, the Boston Red Sox, in the American League Championship Series. The series for the American League pennant proved to be very frustrating to the Yankees, because they had the Red Sox down three games to none. All the Yankees had to do was win one more game, and they would have clinched the pennant and gone on to the World Series. The fourth game in the series was played at Boston's Fenway Park. The Yankees opened the scoring when Rodriguez blasted a two-run homer. In the ninth inning, the Yankees held a one-run lead, but Red Sox pinch runner Dave Roberts stole second and then scored on a single by Bill Mueller. With the score tied, the game went 12 innings with the Red Sox winning on a two-run homer by David Ortiz.

To the dismay of the Yankees and their fans, the Red Sox then took the next three games to win the pennant. It was the first time in the history of Major League Baseball that a team had rallied to win a postseason series after trailing three games to none. The Red Sox went on to sweep the St. Louis Cardinals in the World Series. For Derek and his teammates, losing the American League Championship Series to the Red Sox was a bitter conclusion to what had been another rollercoaster year. Said Derek,

> "You've got to give them credit. The bottom line is we lost. They beat us. We had our opportunities. You've got to make the most of your opportunities and they played better. There's not really much you can do about it. You can't sit here and say, 'This happened, that happened.' I mean, they beat us four games in a row."

For Derek Jeter, helping the team win is more important than individual statistics. "It's simple if you look at it as: Try to win," he said in 2006. "That's the bottom line. If you win, everybody benefits. It's not like, 'I won, I lost.' It's, 'We win, we lost.' That's the only way I've thought about it."

Challenges Ahead

FOLLOWING THE DEVASTATING LOSS TO BOSTON in the 2004 playoffs, Derek Jeter reported to spring training in 2005 determined to lead the Yankees back to the top of the American League. And so when spring training began, he made it clear that other players, specifically Alex Rodriguez, would have to step up and take more responsibility for the team.

Derek wasn't the only member of the Yankees organization who felt Rodriguez could have produced more in 2004. In his first year with the Yankees, Rodriguez hit .286 and slugged 36 homers—decent numbers for most players, but subpar for Rodriguez. After the season, George Steinbrenner talked to Rodriguez, suggesting that he could show more leadership on the field.

An ugly incident during the sixth game of the Red Sox series the previous fall had sparked both Steinbrenner's and Jeter's concern. In the bottom of the eighth, with Derek on first, Rodriguez hit a feeble grounder back to pitcher Bronson Arroyo. Arroyo scooped up the ball and raced over to the baseline, where he reached to tag Rodriguez. But as Arroyo applied the tag, Rodriguez swatted the pitcher's arm, jarring the ball loose. Rodriguez kept running, making it safely to first and heading for second. Meanwhile, during the confusion, Derek rounded the bases and scored all the way from first while Rodriguez took second. At first, the umpires called both players safe. Then, after huddling, they decided Rodriguez had interfered with Arroyo and called him out. Derek was sent back to first, and the Yankees' rally was snuffed out. Rodriguez was loudly criticized by sportswriters and fans for what they regarded as unprofessional play. Arroyo complained after the game,

> "He karate-chopped me. It was so obvious to me. It was a desperate measure at desperate times."

As the 2005 season got underway, Derek was determined to keep his teammates, and particularly Rodriguez, focused on playing hard and fair. He said,

> "That's how you win, you want everyone to go out and play the game the right way. I think if you play the game the right way, that's considered leadership. You don't have to be vocal about it and tell everyone that you're going to do it. You just have to do it."

A Milestone Base Hit

Rodriguez got the message. He posted stellar numbers in 2005, slugging 48 homers and compiling a .321 batting average. What's more, Rodriguez won the Most Valuable Player Award for the American League. But many people felt he harbored some ill will toward Jeter for singling him out for criticism. Said Rodriguez,

> "This is still Jeter's team because he's the captain, but my approach is not to be everyone's best friend. My approach is to win championships. The only way to do that is to be myself, and to take care of my world. With my talent, people will follow naturally."

Derek posted All-Star–caliber numbers in 2005 as well, hitting .309 with 19 homers and 122 runs scored in leading the Yankees to

Challenges Ahead

the American League East title. The Yankees fell in the divisional playoffs, though, and watched the World Series that year at home on TV.

Derek posted impressive numbers in 2006 as well. He just missed winning the American League batting crown, hitting .343, edged out by Joe Mauer of the Minnesota Twins with a .347 average. Derek did reach an impressive milestone in 2006, notching his 2,000th career hit. He became only the eighth Yankee to reach that plateau.

> **CROSS-CURRENTS**
> Read "A New Yankee Stadium" if you want more information about the famous arena where Derek plays his home games. Go to page 52.

Alex Rodriguez (pictured waving after reaching base) has won two Most Valuable Player awards with the New York Yankees. However, Rodriguez is not a popular player in New York. Yankees fans often boo when the all-star third baseman is struggling. By contrast, most fans admire Derek Jeter for his hard play and team-first attitude.

DEREK JETER

    The hit itself was not impressive. With the team trailing the Kansas City Royals at Yankee Stadium, Derek came to bat in the fourth inning against pitcher Scott Elarton. Derek tapped the ball into the dirt, and it was quickly scooped up by catcher Paul Bako, who threw hard to first baseman Doug Mientkiewicz. But the throw sailed high over Mientkiewicz's head and into the stands, allowing Derek to take second base. At first, the official scorer ruled the play

Derek has already proven himself one of the Yankees greatest players. His .316 career batting average ranks fifth on the team's all-time list, behind only Hall of Fame players Babe Ruth (.349), Lou Gehrig (.340), Earle Combs (.325), and Joe DiMaggio (.325). With more than 2,500 career hits, he trails only Gehrig (2,721) in that category.

Challenges Ahead

an error. Then the scorer changed his mind and gave Derek first base on a hit and second base on an error.

The pubic address announcer proclaimed that Derek Jeter had just collected his 2,000th hit, and 48,035 fans in the stands gave the shortstop a rousing ovation. The umpires stopped the game momentarily so that Derek could acknowledge their applause. After the game, Derek said he felt uncomfortable tipping his batting helmet to the crowd because the Yankees were behind at the time and he didn't want to delay play. He said,

> "We were losing at the time, so I didn't really like to do it. But you appreciate how the fans feel. I mean, I wasn't at home, counting down the hits. My job is to get hits and get on base. Getting that many hits only means you've been playing a long time."

Team Chemistry

The Yankees went on to win the American League East in 2006, but, again, they were knocked out of postseason play before the World Series. As the 2007 season got underway, there were obvious ill feelings in the clubhouse, particularly between Jeter and Rodriguez. Earlier in their careers, the two had often hung out together during the off-seasons and had a close relationship. After the 2006 season, Rodriguez had told a magazine interviewer that he thought Jeter was overrated and that he no longer considered the shortstop his friend. Said Rodriguez,

> "People start assuming things are worse than what they are, which they're not. But they are obviously not as great as they used to be, when we were like blood brothers."

Derek tried hard to keep the dispute from affecting team chemistry, but he found himself besieged by sportswriters who wanted to know whether the ill-will would affect the team's play. Finally, Derek declared,

> "What happens off the field has nothing to do with what we're trying to do here."

Despite the hard feelings, Jeter and Rodriguez both posted impressive numbers in 2007. Jeter hit .322 while Rodriguez won another American League MVP award. As for the team, 2007 was another disappointing year. The Red Sox won the Eastern Division. The Yankees made the playoffs as a wild card team but were again knocked out in the first round. At the conclusion of the season, Steinbrenner questioned manager Joe Torre's leadership. The Boss elected not to fire Torre, but offered him only a one-year extension of his contract. Torre rejected the offer and signed on to manage the Los Angeles Dodgers, ending a tenure with the Yankees in which he delivered four World Series titles and five American League pennants.

Derek was saddened by Torre's decision. Torre was the only Major League manager Derek had known. Both men joined the Yankees in the same year, 1996, weathering the team's ups and downs together. Derek said,

> "I have known Mr. Torre for a good majority of my adult life, and there has been no bigger influence on my professional development. It was a privilege to play for him on the field, and an honor to learn from him off the field."

Turn 2 Foundation

Away from baseball, Derek found himself busy with the Turn 2 Foundation. Turn 2 is a charitable organization he established to help young people avoid substance abuse and to reward high achievers—those who, in the language of baseball, pull off a "turn 2," a double play. No. 2 is also the number Derek wears as a Yankee. To manage the day-to-day operations of Turn 2, Derek appointed his father, Charles. The foundation distributes about $1 million a year, which is contributed by Derek as well as other professional athletes and several corporate donors. Derek talked about the difference between his childhood and the young people he tries to help and reward:

> "I started the Turn 2 Foundation for the prevention of substance abuse and promotion of healthy lifestyles for kids. I was fortunate because growing up I had tunnel vision about wanting to play baseball, so I stayed away from drugs and alcohol."

Challenges Ahead

Derek poses with some of the children who benefit from his Turn 2 Foundation. The charitable foundation offers a variety of programs to help young people turn to healthy lifestyles instead of drugs or alcohol. Since the Turn 2 Foundation was established in 1996, it has spent more than $8 million on various youth programs.

Meanwhile, following the 2007 season there were some off-the-field distractions that would prove devastating to the entire sport of baseball. In late 2007, former U.S. Senator George Mitchell issued a report on steroid use in Major League Baseball, finding that many current and former stars used illegal performance-enhancing drugs.

DEREK JETER

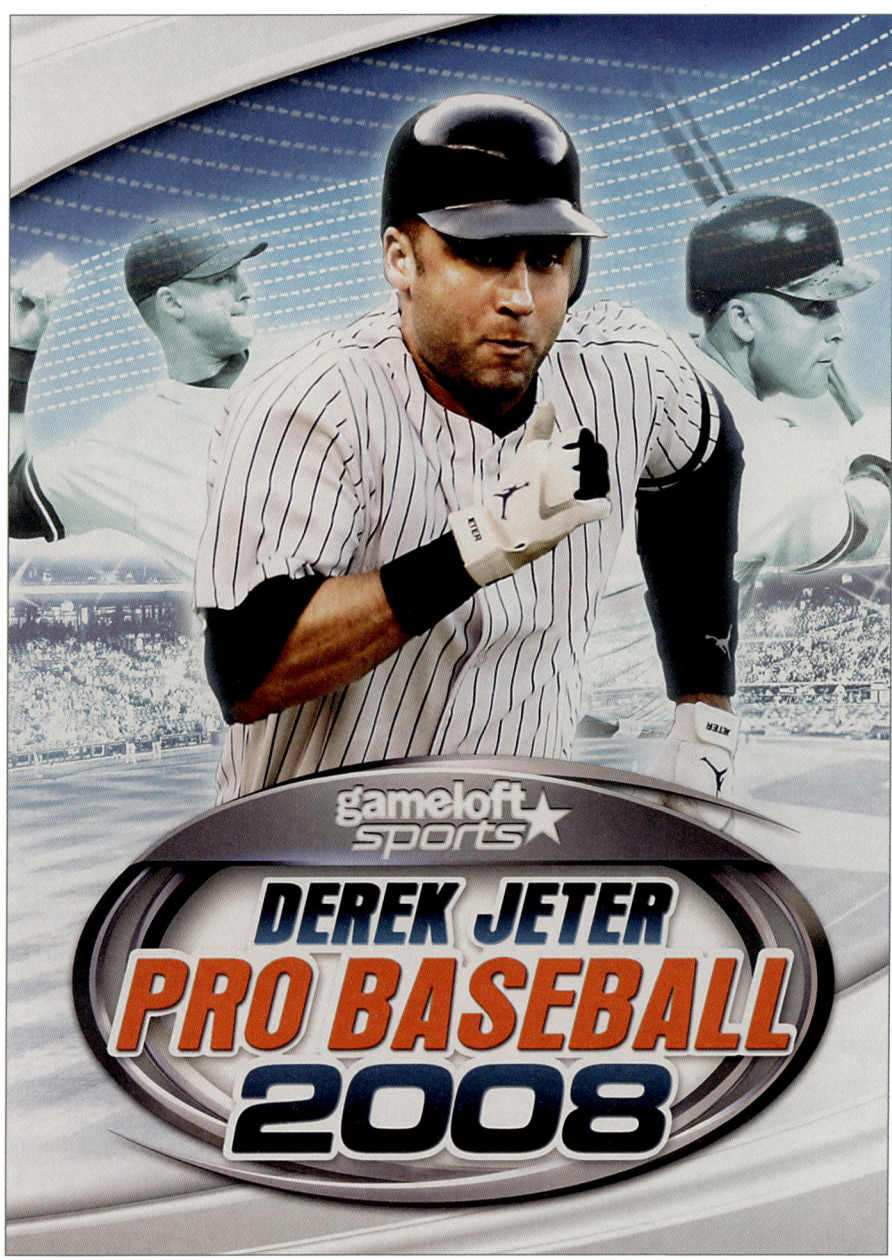

The cover of a popular baseball video game features Derek Jeter. The Yankees captain is respected for his high level of play, his dedication to the team, and his desire to win. Many people also admire Derek because of the classy way in which he conducts himself both on and off the field.

Challenges Ahead

Several Yankees were caught up in the scandal, including pitcher Andy Pettitte, former pitcher Roger Clemens, and designated hitter Jason Giambi. Baseball officials vowed to get tough on the use of steroids, a move opposed by many players and officials of their **union**. Derek has broken ranks on the issue and called for mandatory testing for performance-enhancing drugs. He said,

> "You can test for whatever you want to test for. We get pricked by needles anyway in spring training, so we have a lot of blood work to begin with."

> **CROSS-CURRENTS**
> In recent years, steroid use in baseball has become a controversial issue. To learn more, read "Performance-enhancing Drugs." Go to page 53.

Long Career Ahead

With the steroids scandal hanging over the sport, and with the fortunes of the Yankees in the balance, Derek knows he has a lot of challenges ahead of him as he continues his career. He also knows that he will have to find a way to maintain a healthy relationship with Alex Rodriguez. There is no question that Jeter and Rodriguez are two of the biggest stars in baseball. Together, there may be no limit to what they can accomplish on the field. As adversaries on the same team, though, a deteriorating relationship between the two stars would obviously affect the team's fortunes.

As he continues his career, one fact is certain: Derek Jeter hopes to play for many more years. As some Major League shortstops grow older, they often change positions to extend their careers. Shortstop is a physically demanding position that requires strength, agility, and quickness—attributes often lost as the body ages. But Jeter works hard at staying in shape and says he can see no reason to switch positions. After his contract expires in 2010, he says he hopes to sign a new contract and play many more seasons for the Yankees:

> "That's the plan. I haven't really thought about how long I'm playing. I take it one year at a time; I don't sit down and say, 'Well, I hope I'm playing in two-thousand-whatever.'"

CROSS-CURRENTS

The Subway Series

The 2000 World Series between the Yankees and Mets marked one of the few times in baseball history that two teams from the same city have met in the October classic. Since the World Series was first played in 1903, teams from the same city have met just 16 times. Fourteen of those World Series match-ups featured teams from New York.

The origin of the term "Subway Series" is unknown, but it is believed that New York newspapers used it during the early 1920s as the New York Giants and New York Yankees met in the Series. (The two teams faced each other in 1921, 1922, and 1923.) The term applies to the use of the subway for fans of both teams to attend the games. Whenever a Subway Series has been played in New York, New Yorkers notice an electricity in the air as everyone suddenly becomes a baseball fan. "You kind of felt like that was the way it was supposed to be," said former Brooklyn Dodgers pitcher Joe Black, who played in the Subway Series of 1952 and 1953. "Baseball. New York. Autumn. It all went together."

The First Subway Series

The first Subway Series, played in 1921, featured the Giants and Yankees. All the games were played at the Giants' stadium, the Polo Grounds, because construction of Yankee Stadium had not yet been completed. The teams were headed by two legendary managers: Miller Huggins for the Yankees and John McGraw for the Giants. (Both are in the Baseball **Hall of Fame**.)

The Yankees' best player, Babe Ruth, was hobbled by injuries during the Series, hitting just one home run—after a season in which he set a major-league record with 59. Ruth's limited action hampered the Yankees, who went on to lose the World Series, five games to three. Still, the Yankees established themselves as one of the premier teams in baseball that year by winning their first of 39 American League **pennants**.

Other Subway Match-ups

The 2000 Yankees-Mets match-up was the first Subway Series in New York since 1956, when the Yankees beat the Brooklyn Dodgers two years before the Dodgers moved to Los Angeles. New Yorkers felt that it was about time.

Two other cities have hosted a Subway Series—Chicago in 1906 and St. Louis in 1944. In 1989, the neighboring cities of Oakland and San Francisco hosted the "BART Series," with BART meaning Bay Area Rapid Transit, the public transportation system that links the two cities.

(Go back to page 6.)

CROSS-CURRENTS

Multiracial Americans

With an African American father and white mother, Derek Jeter is one of a growing number of Americans who are born into multiracial households. At one time, multiracial children were largely ignored by society or treated as members of one group or another. In fact, as recently as the 1960s, **miscegenation**, a marriage between people of different races, was against the law in some states. But the **U.S. Supreme Court** ruled in 1967, in the case *Loving v. Virginia*, that all anti-miscegenation laws were unconstitutional.

In 2000, the **U.S. Census Bureau** for the first time allowed Americans to designate themselves as "multiracial" in that year's census. Before 2000, Americans who participated in the census were always asked to designate themselves as members of one specific race. In 2000, more than 7 million Americans, about 2.4 percent of the population, designated themselves as multiracial.

Like Derek, other celebrities are proud of their multiracial heritages. Today, some of the most famous multiracial Americans include politician Barack Obama, news reporter Soledad O'Brian, professional golfer Tiger Woods, pop singers Faith Evans and Mariah Carey, model Tyson Beckford, actresses Halle Berry, Jennifer Beals, Rosario Dawson, Jessica Alba, and Tina and Tamara Mowry, and actors Freddie Prinze Jr., Vin Diesel, and Dwayne "the Rock" Johnson.

During his 2008 campaign for the presidency of the United States, Barack Obama discussed his unusual multiracial background. Obama's parents—a black man from Kenya and a white woman from Kansas—had married early in 1961. In his 1995 memoir Dreams from My Father, *Obama wrote about experiencing racism when he was growing up.*

(Go back to page 12.)

Kalamazoo

Derek Jeter's hometown of Kalamazoo is a small city in southwest Michigan on the banks of the Kalamazoo River. Its name comes from an Indian word meaning "bubbling and boiling water."

Bandleader Glenn Miller made the town famous with his 1942 song, "I've Got a Gal in Kalamazoo." Though there is no zoo in Kalamazoo, there is a vintage airplane museum named the Kalamazoo Air Zoo.

Derek is not the only pro athlete to emerge from Kalamazoo. Others include NFL wide receiver Greg Jennings of the Green Bay Packers, running back T.J. Duckett of the Seattle Seahawks, and Florida Marlins pitcher Scott Olsen.

Derek looks back on his days in Kalamazoo with fondness, and Kalamazoo returns the warm feelings. In 1996, shortly after the Yankees won the World Series, the town honored him by staging Derek Jeter Day. However, Derek admits that playing baseball there could be a challenge:

> "The first thing to know about playing baseball in Michigan is, Michigan's really cold . . . When the season started in March, it would still be raining or sleeting or snowing. The most memorable game of my high school career was at the start of my senior season, one of those drizzly 35-degree March days. I slipped on the slush and sprained my ankle as I rounded first base."

(Go back to page 13.) ◀◀

Visitors to Kalamazoo, Michigan, are greeted by this welcome sign as they enter the city limits. With a population of more than 77,000, Kalamazoo is among the 20 largest cities in Michigan. Since the Yankees drafted Derek Jeter in 1992, the city has been home to two minor-league baseball teams: the Kodiaks (1996–1998) and the Kings (2001–present).

CROSS-CURRENTS

Baseball's High Salaries

Most professional athletes are well paid. But in general, baseball players seem to earn higher salaries than most other pro athletes. Today, the average annual salary for ballplayers is around $3 million.

It was not always this way. Until the mid-1970s, most baseball players earned fairly modest salaries. Their contracts contained language called the "reserve clause." This said that the team controlled the rights to the player. If the player was not happy with the salary he was offered, he could refuse to play, but he was not permitted to sign a deal with another team. The team could trade a player's rights to another team, or sell them for cash. This helped to keep player salaries low.

After the 1969 season, the Philadelphia Phillies tried to trade Richie Allen to the St. Louis Cardinals for All-Star outfielder Curt Flood. Flood refused to go along with the trade, claiming that Major League Baseball had too much control over the lives of the players. Flood filed a lawsuit to challenge baseball's reserve clause, saying,

> "After 12 years in the Major Leagues I do not feel that I am a piece of property to be bought and sold irrespective of my wishes."

Flood lost the case, but his challenge encouraged others. In 1975, pitchers Dave McNally and Andy Messersmith claimed that because they had played a season with no contract, they should be allowed to become free agents and sign with whatever club they chose. An arbitrator hired to settle the dispute ruled in their favor, and the age of free agency in baseball was born. Without the reserve clause, players could now sell their services to the highest bidders once their contracts expired.

In baseball, wealthy owner George Steinbrenner of the Yankees has always been willing to spend whatever it takes to put a winning team on the field. As a result, he pays huge salaries to get top players under Yankee contracts.

Sadly, the one player who never prospered because of the rules change was Flood. After refusing to report to Philadelphia, Flood sat out the 1970 season. He played just 13 games in 1971 before retiring. He died in 1997 at the age of 59, virtually penniless. Said Bill White, a former National League president who had played with Flood in St. Louis,

> "He did something that was courageous, and paid for it—financially, mentally and physically. He changed the thinking, and the change in thinking is much of the reason why we are where we are."

(Go back to page 18.)

CROSS-CURRENTS

George Steinbrenner—Always the Boss

Known as the "Boss," George Steinbrenner is one of baseball's most controversial owners. A billionaire who made his fortune in the shipbuilding business, Steinbrenner is willing to spend whatever it takes to lure the best talent to the Yankees. He has also gained a reputation as one of baseball's most dictatorial owners.

That reputation earned him his nickname. Indeed, after Steinbrenner bought the Yankees in 1973, he hired and fired 20 managers in 23 years before settling into a long-term relationship with Joe Torre from 1996 through the 2007 season, when Torre left New York rather than accept a limited one-year contract with much of his salary dependent on achieving specific goals in the post-season.

Generally, Steinbrenner has maintained a good relationship with Derek, but even that has been marked by tensions. In 2002 he heard Derek had been out late to a party the night before a game and snapped that his shortstop "better pay more attention to the ball game than he does the women." While comments like these are provocative and brash, they are so typical of Steinbrenner's style that they have become part of the story of the sorts of pressures players must endure if they are to play for the Yankees. Later, Steinbrenner and Derek made a Visa credit card commercial together, where they poked fun at their spat.

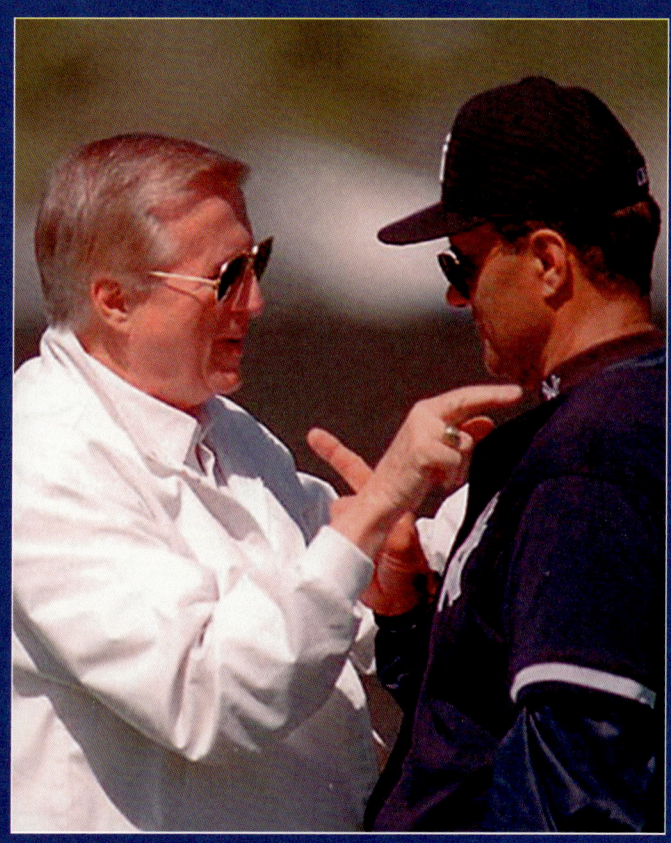

After buying the Yankees in 1973, George Steinbrenner (left) became heavily involved in the day-to-day management of the team. Steinbrenner has often clashed with his team's managers, including Joe Torre (right). In recent years, however, Steinbrenner has taken a less active role. His sons Hal and Hank have taken over most of the decision-making.

(Go back to page 18.)

The Hottest Sports Rivalries

The rivalry between the Boston Red Sox and New York Yankees is one of the longest and most heated in sports. The rivalry dates back to 1920 when the Sox—at the time one of the most dominant teams in the American League, having won five World Series—traded Babe Ruth to the Yankees. Ruth led the Yankees to seven World Series titles over the next 12 years, while the Red Sox never won the World Series again until 2004.

One particularly bitter defeat for Boston fans came in 1978. In July of that season, the Sox led the Yankees by 14 games. However, a late-season surge by the Yankees meant that the teams finished the season tied for the AL East title. A one-game playoff was held to determine the division champion, and the Yankees won. New York went on to win the World Series.

Hot and Getting Hotter

Over the past few decades the rivalry has heated up, and fans of the teams have grown increasingly hostile. Harvey Frommer, co-author of the book *Red Sox Vs. Yankees: The Great Rivalry*, believes the hostility is partly geographic. The cities are 190 miles apart and have long been the only American League teams in the northeastern United States. Also, Frommer says, the hostility may be related to the idea held by many Bostonians that New Yorkers feel superior because their city is so much larger. He said,

> "You've got this monster city of New York going against the second-city, or third-city, complex. You also have all these transplanted New Yorkers living in Boston and transplanted Bostonians in New York. The cities are very close together."

Other Historic Rivalries

There are many other famous professional sports rivalries. The Toronto Maple Leafs and Montreal Canadiens have competed head to head since the earliest days of the National Hockey League. To Canadian fans, the teams represented the best of English Canada (Toronto) against the best of French Canada (Montreal). The Leafs and Canadiens have met five times in the Stanley Cup finals.

Football is also full of intense regional and divisional rivalries. One of the longest and most famous is between the Chicago Bears and Green Bay Packers. These two franchises are two of the oldest, most established teams in the National Football League. Separated by about the same distance along Lake Michigan as New York and Boston are along the Atlantic Seaboard, Green Bay and Chicago fans share geography and a passionate dislike of the other city's team.

(Go back to page 30.)

CROSS-CURRENTS

A New Yankee Stadium

The exterior of Yankee Stadium in the Bronx, perhaps the most famous ballpark in the world. The ballpark was built in 1923, and seats more than 57,000 fans. In July 2008, Major League Baseball's All-Star game was held at Yankee Stadium, as a way to honor the historic ballpark in its final season.

When Derek Jeter takes the field in 2009, chances are he will be playing in a new Yankee Stadium. That spring, after nearly nine decades of playing their home games in the old stadium, the Yankees will move out of baseball's most hallowed ballpark and into a new $1.3 billion facility.

Located in the New York City borough of the Bronx, Yankee Stadium opened in 1923. Until then, the Yankees had been sharing another stadium, the Polo Grounds, with the New York Giants of the National League. But in 1920, the Yankees outdrew the Giants in attendance, thanks to the acquisition of Babe Ruth. Bitter that the Yankees were outdrawing them in their own ballpark, the Giants told the Yankees to find a new place to play. Because Yankee Stadium was built as a result of one player's popularity, the new ballpark was nicknamed "the House that Ruth Built." (As for the Giants, they eventually left New York for San Francisco.)

Since 1923, Yankee Stadium has hosted 37 World Series—more than any other ballpark. For many years, the stadium also served as home for the New York Giants of the NFL, until the Giants moved into their own stadium in 1974. The new Yankee Stadium has been built adjacent to the old ballpark, which will be demolished when the new park opens. (Go back to page 39.) ⏪

Performance-enhancing Drugs

Athletes taking massive amounts of steroids find that the drug can help them run faster, lift heavier weights, throw harder, and maintain their endurance for longer periods. Steroids convert into the male hormone testosterone when they are injected, which helps the body convert protein into muscle mass. The typical male body produces about ten milligrams of testosterone a day, but athletes who abuse steroids inject doses that produce hundreds of milligrams a day.

However, long-term use of steroids has a devastating effect on the body, causing bloating, weight gain, blood-clotting disorders, liver damage, premature heart attacks and stroke, high blood pressure, weak tendons, high cholesterol, addiction dependence, acne, kidney disease, cancer, and a personality disorder known as 'Roid Rage.

Moving Steroids to the National Stage

Steroids and other performance-enhancing drugs became a major issue in baseball in 2005 when former big-league slugger Jose Canseco published *Juiced: Wild Times, Rampant 'Roids, Smash Hits, and How Baseball Got Big*. In the book Canseco, who had hit 462 home runs during his career, admitted that he had used steroids and claimed that many other players had as well during the 1990s.

Soon after the book was published, the U.S. House Government Reform Committee convened a hearing in Washington to investigate the use of steroids in sports. Canseco and other top players, including Sammy Sosa and Mark McGwire, testified at the hearing. In 1998, McGwire and Sosa had both broken Roger Maris's longtime record of 61 home runs in a season: Sosa hit 66 homers that year while McGwire slugged 70. Both men have denied charges that they had used steroids to enhance their athletic abilities. However, others have challenged those denials.

How Rampant Are 'Roids?

After Canseco's revelations, Major League Baseball retained former U.S. Senator George Mitchell to investigate the use of steroids in baseball. In late 2007, Mitchell issued a 406-page report alleging that steroid use remains rampant in baseball. His report named 86 prominent current and former players who are believed to have used steroids, including Barry Bonds, the career home run leader.

Steroid abuse has touched other sports as well. In 2008, sprinter Marion Jones began serving a prison term of six months for lying to investigators when she said she didn't use steroids during the 2000 Olympic Games in Sydney, Australia. As a result of the scandal, Jones was forced to return the three gold medals and two bronze medals she won at the Olympics. Two prominent athletes, football player Lyle Alzado and baseball star Ken Caminiti, died after years of steroid abuse.

(Go back to page 45.)

CHRONOLOGY

1974 Derek Jeter is born June 26 in Pequannock, New Jersey.

1991 Hits .557 as a junior at Kalamazoo Central High School, drawing the attention of Major League scouts.

1992 Selected sixth overall in the amateur baseball draft on June 1 by the New York Yankees.

1993 Playing for a Yankees farm team in Greensboro, North Carolina, commits 56 errors in his first full season of professional baseball.

1996 Opens the season as Yankees starting shortstop on April 2 and hits a home run in his first game; later, selected American League Rookie of the Year.

1998 Begins a relationship with Mariah Carey, his first of many romantic encounters with beautiful actresses, models, and singers.

2000 Named Most Valuable Player of the All-Star Game and World Series.

2001 Signs a $189 million contract with the Yankees; late in the year, during a postseason game on Oct. 13 against the Oakland Athletics, Jeter executes the miraculous play in the field known as "The Flip."

2003 In a game against the Toronto Blue Jays on March 31, the opening day of the season, dislocates his shoulder and misses nearly two months of the season.

2004 Derek wins his first Gold Glove award as the league's best-fielding shortstop.

2006 Records his 2,000th career hit in a May 26 game against the Kansas City Royals.

2007 Derek hits .322 and scores 102 runs.

2008 Derek Jeter is voted to the All-Star team for the ninth time.

ACCOMPLISHMENTS & AWARDS

1992 Kalamazoo Area B'nai B'rith Award for Scholar Athlete
American Baseball Coaches Association High School Player of the Year
Gatorade High School Athlete of the Year
USA Today High School Player of the Year
Selected sixth overall by New York Yankees in the June 1992 draft

1993 South Atlantic League Most Outstanding Major League Prospect
South Atlantic League All-Star Team
Baseball America South Atlantic League Best Defensive Shortstop, Most Exciting Player and Best Infield Arm

1994 *Baseball America* Minor League Player of the Year
The Sporting News Minor League Player of the Year
USA Today Baseball Weekly Minor League Player of the Year
Topps/North American Professional Baseball League Minor League Player of the Year
Florida State League Most Valuable Player

1995 International League All-Star Team

1996 American League Rookie of the Year

1998 American League All-Star Team

1999 American League All-Star Team

2000 American League All-Star Team
Most Valuable Player, All-Star Game
Most Valuable Player, World Series
Baseball Writers Association of America Babe Ruth Award for Best Performance in the World Series

2001 "The Flip" named by *USA Today* as one of top ten baseball plays at all time.
American League All-Star Team

2002 American League All-Star Team

2003 Named New York Yankees captain

2004 American League All-Star Team
Gold Glove
"The Dive" voted Play of the Year by fans at MLB.com.

ACCOMPLISHMENTS & AWARDS

2005   Gold Glove

2006   Gold Glove
Silver Slugger
Hank Aaron Award for Best Overall Hitter in Baseball
MLB.com Hitter of the Year Award
The Sporting News All-Star Shortstop
American League All-Star Team

2007   Silver Slugger
American League All-Star Team

FURTHER READING & INTERNET RESOURCES

Books

Jeter, Derek. *Game Day: My Life On and Off the Field*. New York: Three Rivers Press, 2001.

Jeter, Derek, and Jack Curry. *The Life You Imagine: Life Lessons For Achieving Your Dreams*. New York: Crown Publishers, 2002.

Mills, Clifford W. *Derek Jeter*. New York: Checkmark Books, 2008.

Pitoniak, Scott. *Memories of Yankee Stadium*. Chicago: Triumph Books, 2008.

Robinson, Tom. *Derek Jeter: Captain On and Off the Field*. Berkeley Heights, N.J.: Enslow Publishers, 2006.

Web Sites

http://www.mlb.com/players/jeter_derek/index.jsp
Official Web site for Derek Jeter. Visitors can read a biography of Jeter, read the on-line journal he keeps during the season, scan his statistics, and see videos of some of his extraordinary plays.

http://newyork.yankees.mlb.com/index.jsp?c_id=nyy
Official Web site for the New York Yankees. Visitors can review the Yankees roster, check the schedule and read news reports on the team. Visitors can also find a history of Yankee Stadium and receive updates on construction of the new stadium, set to open in 2009.

http://mlb.mlb.com/
Major League Baseball maintains this Web site so fans can follow the sport as well as developments in the thirty teams of the American and National leagues. By accessing the "Player Search" feature, fans can find news and statistics on every player in the Major Leagues.

http://www.kalamazoocity.org/
Web site maintained by the city of Kalamazoo, Michigan. Visitors can find information about the history of Kalamazoo as well as the city's government and social activities.

http://academic.udayton.edu/race/01race/multi01.htm
Website maintained by the Law School of the University of Dayton in Ohio, outlining the history and background of laws in the United States that have recognized the rights of multiracial Americans. Legal scholars have contributed essays to the site on such issues as racism, poverty, housing, and employment.

FURTHER READING & INTERNET RESOURCES

http://www.pbs.org/newshour/bb/remember/1997/flood_1-21.html
Companion Web site to the PBS *NewsHour* feature "Changing the Rules," which reported on the life of Curt Flood, the Major League player who challenged baseball's Reserve Clause. Visitors to the site can read about Flood's life and the legal challenge that resulted in free agency in baseball.

http://mlb.mlb.com/mlb/news/mitchell/index.jsp
Web site maintained by Major League Baseball giving access to the report by former Senator George Mitchell on the use of performance enhancing drugs in baseball. Visitors to the site can download the report.

Publisher's note:
The Web sites mentioned in this book were active at the time of publication. The publisher is not responsible for Web sites that have changed their addresses or discontinued operation since the date of publication. The publisher will review and update the Web site addresses each time the book is reprinted.

GLOSSARY

American League—established in 1901, league of baseball clubs that now includes the Baltimore Orioles, Boston Red Sox, Chicago White Sox, Cleveland Indians, Detroit Tigers, Kansas City Royals, Los Angeles Angels, Minnesota Twins, New York Yankees, Oakland Athletics, Seattle Mariners, Tampa Bay Devil Rays, Texas Rangers, Toronto Blue Jays.

coat of arms—dating back to medieval times, decoration a knight wore on his armor; the coat of arms often featured symbols of significance to the knight, such as illustrations displaying his bravery or achievements in battle.

contract—legal agreement between two parties, often requiring one side to pay the other to perform certain services over a specified period of time.

farm system—system of minor league teams in which young players are given the opportunity to develop their skills before moving up to a Major League team.

Hall of Fame—in baseball, the institution in Cooperstown, New York, that honors the game's best players.

humerus—longest bone in the arm, extending from the shoulder to the elbow.

immortal—ability to live forever; often refers to the reputation of political leaders, athletes, and other celebrities whose deeds are remembered throughout time.

inning—the portion of the game of baseball in which each side is given a chance to score; each side's share of the inning—the top and the bottom—is over after the players make three outs. Horseshoes and cricket are also played in innings.

journalists—professionals who report and write news for newspapers, magazines, radio and TV broadcasts, and Internet outlets.

miscegenation—literally, "mixture of races." The term is used to refer to a marriage or union involving two people of different races.

National League—founded in 1876, league of baseball clubs that now includes the Arizona Diamondbacks, Atlanta Braves, Chicago Cubs, Cincinnati Reds, Colorado Rockies, Florida Marlins, Houston Astros, Los Angeles Dodgers, Milwaukee Brewers, New York Mets, Philadelphia Phillies, Pittsburgh Pirates, St. Louis Cardinals, San Diego Padres, San Francisco Giants, and Washington Nationals,.

pennants—the flags won by the champions of the American and National leagues, which are flown over their home ballparks.

rookie—in sports, a first-year player.

GLOSSARY

sacrifice fly—ball hit in the air in which an outfielder makes an easy out, but the ball is hit deep enough to allow a base runner to tag the base after the catch and then advance a base or score; the hitter has "sacrificed" himself by making an out that benefits his team.

scholarship—financial aid provided by a college or university to a student to recognize the student's academic or athletic abilities; some athletic scholarships enable talented athletes to receive a free education in return for playing for the school's interscholastic sports teams.

shortstop—the infielder who is stationed between second and third base; strategically, one of the most important positions on the field because most hitters are right-handed and tend to drive the ball toward left field, which is blocked by the shortstop to cut off their hits.

subway—underground rail transportation system found in many major cities.

tabloid—style of journalism that concentrates on scandal, celebrity news, and sensational crime; named for tabloid-sized newspapers, which are different in size and format from broadsheet newspapers.

union—organization that represents workers in their negotiations with a corporation; during negotiations, the union presents the workers' demands for pay and other work-related issues.

U.S. Census Bureau—agency of the federal government charged with discovering and reporting the size and social characteristics of the U.S. population.

U.S. Supreme Court—one of the three branches of the federal government, the most powerful court in America; usually restricts itself to determining whether laws conform with the principles established by the U.S. Constitution.

NOTES

page 6 "I basically had the same . . ." Thomas Hill, "Jeter's Star of Stars: MVP Raps Three Hits in AL Win," *New York Daily News* (July 12, 2000), p. 58.

page 9 "Going into Shea Stadium . . ." Derek Jeter, *Game Day: My Life On and Off the Field* (New York: Three Rivers Press, 2001), p. 83.

page 9 "Winning the MVP award . . ." Jeter, *Game Day*, p. 83.

page 12 "My mother and father are . . ." Derek Jeter and Jack Curry, *The Life You Imagine: Life Lessons for Achieving Your Dreams* (New York: Crown Publishers, 2000), p. xxii.

page 12 "He was pretty much head . . ." Buster Olney, "Derek Jeter: The Pride of Kalamazoo," *New York Times* (April 4, 1999), p. 8-1.

page 13 "He's like a colt . . ." Jon Heyman, "A Ways to Go: Yanks' Jeter Raw but Making Strides," *Newsday* (March 15, 1993), p. 84.

page 15 "The Yankees, who had been . . ." Jeter and Curry, *The Life You Imagine*, p. 11.

page 18 "Derek Jeter embodies everything . . ." Ronald Blum, "Jeter, Yankees Finalize Contract: $189 Million, 10-Year Deal 2nd Richest in Sports History," *Pittsburgh Post-Gazette* (February 10, 2001), p. B-1.

page 20 "I really felt there was . . ." "N.Y. Yankees' Star Derek Jeter Inks Second-Highest Sports Contract in History," *Jet* 99, no. 11 (February 26, 2001), p. 51.

page 22 "There are players in . . ." Filip Bondy, "Jeter Runs to Ball, Picks It Up and Flips to Place in History," *New York Daily News* (October 14, 2001), p. 52.

page 23 "They kept battling . . ." Adam Rubin, "Jeter Still Can't Believe It's Over," *New York Daily News* (November 5, 2001), p. 12.

page 25 "It's hard for me to . . ." Michael Silver, "Prince of the City," *Sports Illustrated* 90, no. 25 (June 21, 1999), p. 88.

page 28 "A shoulder dislocation is . . ." Greg Gittrich, "Yankees' Jeter Out at Least Six Weeks: MRI Tomorrow in Florida," *New York Daily News* (April 2, 2003), p. 9.

page 28 "The reality in that clubhouse . . ." Tyler Kepner, "Steinbrenner Appoints Jeter Captain of the Yankees," *New York Times* (June 4, 2003), p. D-1.

page 31 "There's no way you can . . ." Tyler Kepner, "Disappointed Jeter Sounds a Little Bit Like His Employer," *New York Times* (October 28, 2003), p. D-1.

page 31 "Jeter's good. . ." Jeff Merron, "The List: Most Overrated Athletes," ESPN Page 2, http://espn.go.com/page2/s/list/most overrated.html.

page 32 "Those are the things . . ." Dom Amore, "Dive Bomber: Jeter Saves Tie Before Rally in the 13th," *Hartford Courant* (July 2, 2004), p. C-1.

page 32 "I'd have to change my . . ." Tyler Kepner, "Jeter's Skid is a Mystery With Few Clues," *New York Times* (May 25, 2004), p. D-1.

page 35 "You've got to give them . . ." Christian Red, "Jeter: Boston's Curse Not Reversed," *Pittsburgh Post-Gazette* (October 25, 2004), p. D-5.

page 36 "It's simple if you . . ." Tyler Kepner, "Jeter's Secret? It's Simple: Play to Win," *New York Times* (August 18, 2006), p. C1.

NOTES

page 38 "He karate-chopped me . . ." Jack O'Connell, "Long Arm of Law Slaps A-Rod; Interference Call Stops Rally in the 8th," *Hartford Courant* (October 20, 2004), p. C-6.

page 38 "That's how you win . . ." Anthony McCarron, "Captain Pilots Yanks Peace: Invites A-Rod to be a Leader, Too," *New York Daily News* (February 9, 2005), p. 78.

page 38 "This is still Jeter's team . . ." McCarron, "Captain Pilots Yanks Peace," p. 78.

page 41 "We were losing at the time . . ." John Altavilla, "K.C. Ends Bronx Bomb; First Win Since 2002. Jeter Gets 2,000th Hit," *Hartford Courant* (May 27, 2006), p. C-1.

page 41 "People start assuming things . . ." Quoted in Jim Baumbach, "Spring Training, Estranged Bedfellows, A-Rod: No More Sleepovers with Jeter, but the Two Co-Exist," *Newsday* (February 20, 2007), p. A-66.

page 41 "What happens off the field . . ." Dom Amore, "'He Knows I Still Support Him,' But Jeter Downplays Off-Field Friendship," *Hartford Courant* (February 21, 2007), p. C-2.

page 42 "I have known Mr. Torre . . ." Kat O'Brien, "Jeter: Torre a 'Friend for Life,'" *Newsday* (October 24, 2007), p. A-51.

page 42 "I started the Turn 2 . . ." Derek Jeter and Elyssa Lee, "Sacrifice Guy," *InStyle* 11, no. 10 (September 2004), p. 542.

page 45 "You can test for whatever . . ." Mason Levinson and Scott Soshnick, "Jeter Says Blood-Testing of Ballplayers Wouldn't Be Intrusive," Bloomberg.com (February 22, 2008). http://www.bloomberg.com/apps/news?pid=20601079&refer=home&sid=aXEs5WaDxwnc.

page 45 "That's the plan . . ." Mark Feinsand, "Captain Makes Position Clear," *New York Daily News* (February 23, 2008), p. 41.

page 48 "The first thing to know . . ." Derek Jeter, "Kalamazoo Kid," *Sports Illustrated* 100, no. 5 (February 9, 2004), p. 39.

page 49 "After 12 years in . . ." Sandy Grady, "The Man Who Changed the Game," *USA Today* (April 3, 2007), p. A-15.

page 49 "He did something that was . . ." Steve Jacobson, "His Fight for Freedom Cost Him Dearly," *Newsday* (January 21, 1997), p. A-62.

page 51 "You've got this monster city . . ." Mike Dodd, "Red Sox vs. Yankees: Bitter Enemies Clash With Series on the Line," *USA Today* (October 11, 2004). http://www.usatoday.com/sports/baseball/playoffs/2004-10-11-cover-rivalry_x.htm.

INDEX

All-Star Game, **4**, 5–6
American League Rookie of the Year award, 15, 17
Arroyo, Bronson, 37–38

Boston Red Sox, 29–30, 31, 35, 37–38, 42, 51
Boyer, Clete, 13

Carey, Mariah, 25, 47
Cashman, Brian, 28
charity work, 42–43
Clemens, Roger, 22, 45

DiMaggio, Joe, 6, **40**
"The Dive," 31–32

"The Flip," 21–22

Garciaparra, Nomar, 5, 18
Gehrig, Lou, 6, 28, **40**
Giambi, Jason, 27, 45
Giambi, Jeremy, 20
Glashow, Jonathan, 28

Huckaby, Ken, 27–28

Jackson, Reggie, 6
Jeter, Charles (father), 11–12, 42
Jeter, Derek
  and the All-Star Game MVP award, **4**, 5–6
  awards and honors won by, **4**, 9, 13, 15, 17, 31
  birth and childhood, 10–12
  and celebrity, 24–25
  and charity work, 42–43
  defensive play of, **8**, 20–22, 31–32
  and earnings, 17–18, 20
  and injuries, **26**, 27–28
  is drafted by the New York Yankees, 13
  at Kalamazoo Central High School, 12–13, **14**
  in the minor leagues, 13, 15
  and multiracial heritage, 47
  with the New York Yankees, 15, 17–23, 27–35, 37–42, 45
  as New York Yankees captain, 28–29, 37–38
  and romantic relationships, 25
  statistics, 17, **34**, 38–39
  2,000th career hit, 39–41
  and the World Series MVP award, 9
  See also New York Yankees
Jeter, Dorothy (mother), 11–12
Jeter, Sharlee (sister), 11–12

Kalamazoo, MI, 12–13, **14**, 48

Leiter, Al, 6, 9
Long, Terrence, 20, 22

Mantle, Mickey, 6
Martinez, Tino, 9, 20, 22
Mattingly, Don, 28
Merron, Jeff, 31
Mitchell, George, 43, 53
Munson, Thurman, 28
Mussina, Mike, 22

Nettles, Graig, 28
New York Yankees, 15, 17–23, 27–35, 37–42, 45, 51, 52
  draft Jeter, 13
  and Jeter as captain, 28–29, 37–38
  and team chemistry, 41–42, 45
  and the World Series, 6–7, 9, 15, 17, 18, **19**, 22–23, 30–31, 46
  See also Jeter, Derek

Oosterbaan, Chris, 12

Pettitte, Andy, 45
Posada, Jorge, 20

Randolph, Willie, 28
Rodriguez, Alex, 5–6, **16**, 18, 32, **33**, 35, 37–38, 41–42, 45
Ruth, Babe, 6, 28, **40**, 46, 51, 52

salaries, baseball, 49
Soriano, Alfonso, 20
Spencer, Shane, 20
Steinbrenner, George, 18, 28, 37, 42, 49, 50
steroids, 43, 45, 53

Tarasco, Tony, 15
Torre, Joe, 15, 28, 32, 42, 50
Turn 2 Foundation, 42–43

University of Michigan, 13
USA Today High School Player of the Year, 13

Washington, Ron, 20
Winfield, Dave, 6
World Series, 6–7, 9, 15, 17, 18, **19**, 22–23, 30–31, 46

Yankee Stadium, 52
  See also New York Yankees

Numbers in ***bold italics*** refer to captions.

ABOUT THE AUTHOR

Hal Marcovitz has written more than 100 books for young readers. He lives in Chalfont, Pennsylvania, with his wife, Gail, and daughter, Ashley. He has also written about Venus and Serena Williams in the MODERN ROLE MODELS series.

PICTURE CREDITS

page
- **1:** MLB Photos/SPCS
- **4:** Steve Schaefer/AFP Photos
- **7:** Sports Illustrated/NMI
- **8:** Tringali Jr./SportsChrome Pix
- **10:** ASP Library
- **14:** New Millennium Images
- **16:** Sports Illustrated/NMI
- **19:** J.V. Lovero/Sports Illustrated/SPCS
- **21:** Contra Costa Times/KRT
- **23:** Newsday/KRT
- **24:** Keith Allison/SPCS
- **26:** Keith Allison/SPCS
- **29:** Keith Allison/SPCS
- **30:** Newsday/KRT
- **33:** G. Simmons/SPCS
- **34:** Sports Illustrated/NMI
- **36:** Keith Allison/SPCS
- **39:** Kansas City Star/MCT
- **40:** MLB Photos/SPCS
- **43:** Chuck Comer/Time Inc./PRMS
- **44:** Gameloft/NMI
- **47:** Newswire/PRMS
- **48:** Denny's/IOA Photos
- **50:** Newsday/KRT
- **52:** Kjetil Ree/SPCS

Front cover: MLB Photos/SPCS

Prospect Heights Public Library
12 N. Elm Street
Prospect Heights, IL 60070
www.phpl.info